Flying the Sky

Passenger Planes

Wendy Hinote Lanier

AV2

www.av2books.com

Step 1
Go to **www.av2books.com**

Step 2
Enter this unique code

PCQRKLZ0A

Step 3
Explore your interactive eBook!

CONTENTS

AV2 is optimized for use on any device

Your interactive eBook comes with...

Contents
Browse a live contents page to easily navigate through resources

Audio
Listen to sections of the book read aloud

Videos
Watch informative video clips

Weblinks
Gain additional information for research

Try This!
Complete activities and hands-on experiments

Key Words
Study vocabulary, and complete a matching word activity

Quizzes
Test your knowledge

Slideshows
View images and captions

... and much, much more!

Passenger Planes

Contents

Chapter 1

At the Airport

Passenger planes carry people to and from places all over the world.

A family arrives at the airport. It is early morning. Many people are already there. The people will travel all over the world. First, they wait in line to **check** their bags. Then, they go through **security**. Next, they find their gate. They wait there until it is time to board the plane.

More than 800 million people passed through U.S. airport security in 2018.

On the plane, people find their seats. They watch out the windows as luggage is loaded onto the plane. Then, it is time for takeoff. The plane zooms down the runway. Soon, it lifts off the ground. It flies high above the clouds.

To board a plane, passengers walk through a tunnel called a jet bridge.

Chapter 2

Bigger, Faster, Farther

A Douglas DC3 flies over a transatlantic liner in New York in 1938.

The Boeing 307 carried 33 passengers and a 5-person crew.

The airplane was invented in 1903. Over the next 30 years, a few small planes carried passengers. Then **airliners** were invented. The Douglas DC-3 was a famous airliner. It carried 21 passengers. People could travel faster and farther than ever before. For this reason, the DC-3 is known as the plane that changed the world.

The Boeing 307 appeared in 1940. It was the first passenger plane with a **pressurized** cabin. The plane could fly above the clouds. That meant it could avoid bad weather.

In the 1950s, passenger planes began using jet engines. These engines made the planes fly faster. The DH-106 Comet and Boeing 707 were the first passenger jets. These jets made air travel easier. Companies could fly more people for less money.

The Boeing 747 was introduced in 1969. It used **turbofan engines** and could hold up to 450 people. The 747 became one of the most successful jets ever built. It is still used today.

Flying in Comfort

Before 1940, airplanes did not fly higher than 10,000 feet (3,050 meters). Air above this height has less oxygen. It is harder for people to breathe. Pressurized cabins keep the air inside the plane similar to the air on the ground. That way, the plane can fly high without hurting passengers.

Chapter 3

Getting Into the Air

In the cockpit, the pilots work together to fly the plane.

Passenger planes come in several sizes. However, most planes have the same basic parts. An airplane's body is called the fuselage. The cockpit is at the front of the fuselage. The pilots sit in this area. The cabin is behind the cockpit. Passengers sit in the cabin.

During takeoff, parts called flaps stick out from the back of the wings. Flaps help create more lift.

The wings are the most important part of an airplane. The shape of the wings creates lift. Lift is an upward force. It causes the plane to rise up into the air. At the same time, **thrust** moves the airplane forward. Most passenger planes use engines to create thrust.

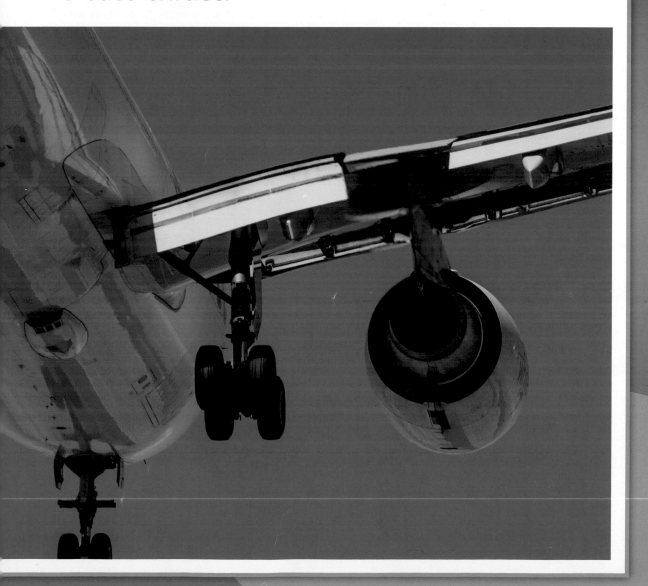

Smaller planes may have only one engine. Large planes have two to four. Most planes use jet engines, but a few use propellers.

Wing Shape

The back of an airplane wing comes to a sharp edge. The front of the wing is thicker and rounded. The wing's top is curved. Because of this shape, air flowing over the top of the wing creates low air pressure. High pressure under the wing can push the plane up.

The plane's tail provides balance. It is also used to steer the plane. The tail has two parts. One is the horizontal **stabilizer**. This part moves the plane up or down. The other part is the vertical stabilizer. This part moves the plane to the left or right.

The flaps on the horizontal stabilizers are called elevators. The flap on the vertical stabilizer is called the rudder.

Parts of a Plane

cockpit

fuselage

jet engine

vertical stabilizer

wing

horizontal stabilizer

Chapter 4

Air Travel Today

About 5,000 aircraft are flying in the United States at a time.

Millions of people travel in airplanes every day. They can go long distances in just a few hours. Computers help plan the plane's route. Some even help the pilots fly the plane.

In most planes, the cockpit is the size of a car. That way, the pilots can reach all the controls. The displays are easy to read and use. Every light and switch has a specific purpose. Some tell the pilots about **flight conditions**. Some warn about possible problems.

A Giant Jet

The Airbus A380 is the largest passenger plane in the world. This double-deck plane has two levels of seats. It can carry more than 800 people. Four turbofan engines power the huge plane. It can go more than 9,000 miles (14,500 kilometers) in a single trip.

The autopilot feature was first invented in 1912.

Airplane cabins must meet safety standards. Seatbelts protect passengers if there is a crash. There are lights along the floor of the cabin. The lights show the way to exit the plane.

Seats in the cabin often have touchscreens on their backs.

An airplane evacuation slide can fully inflate in six seconds.

Plane crashes are rare. In fact, flying is one of the safest ways to travel. People continue to improve airplanes. They collect information about many planes and airports. They study **flight patterns** as well. This information helps them create better designs. The new planes are even safer. They will carry passengers all over the world.

Turbofan Engines

Today, most passenger planes have turbofan engines. The engines are inside large tubes. A huge fan sits at the front of each tube. The fan sends air through and around the engine. In passenger planes, the fans send most of the air around the engines. Less air goes through the center.

Scientists continue to design better turbofan engines.

Sending air around the engines cools and quiets them. This helps them use less fuel. It also produces more thrust. The air that goes through the engine's center is mixed with fuel and burned. This creates power to drive the fans.

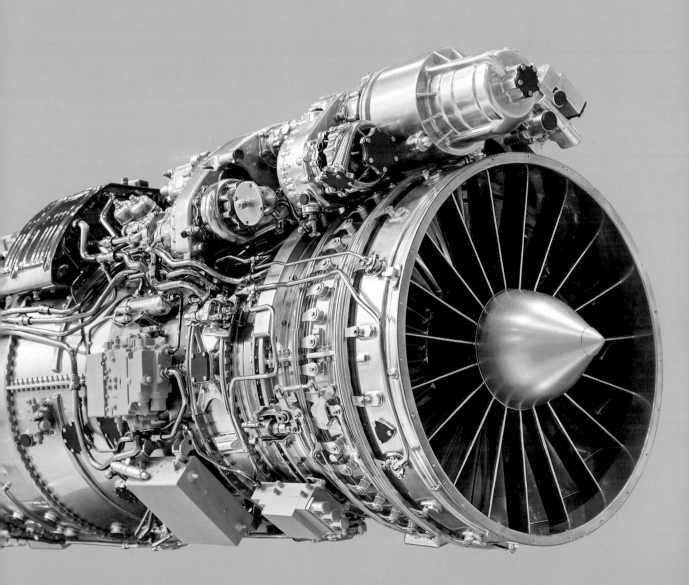

Fun Facts

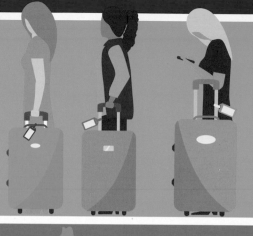

In the United States, more than 2 million people travel on airplanes each day.

The DC-3 could go more than 190 miles per hour (306 km/h). It could fly across the United States in 16 hours.

Propeller planes fly lower and slower than jets. However, they can land on shorter runways.

A Boeing 747 has 365 switches, dials, and lights in its cockpit.

Quiz

1 How many aircraft are flying in the U.S. at one time?

2 What was the first passenger plane to have a pressurized cabin?

3 Why do turbofan engines send air around the engine?

4 Where do the pilots sit in a passenger plane?

5 What is the largest passenger plane in the world?

6 In what year was the airplane invented?

Answers: 1. About 5,000 **2.** The Boeing 307 **3.** To cool and quiet them, use less fuel, and produce more thrust **4.** The cockpit **5.** The Airbus A380 **6.** 1903

Key Words

airliners: large, metal airplanes used for carrying passengers

check: to send bags separately rather than carrying them onto the plane

flight conditions: details including the air temperature and weather around an airplane as it flies

flight patterns: steps for takeoff, landing, and flight of various aircraft

pressurized: brought to an air pressure that is comfortable for breathing

security: a part of an airport where passengers and their bags are checked to make sure they are not carrying anything dangerous

stabilizer: a part of an airplane that the moving parts of the tail are attached to

thrust: a force that pushes air backwards and causes an airplane to move forward

turbofan engines: jet engines that use a large fan to help produce more power

Index

Get the best of both worlds.

AV2 bridges the gap between print and digital.

The expandable resources toolbar enables quick access to content including **videos**, **audio**, **activities**, **weblinks**, **slideshows**, **quizzes**, and **key words**.

Animated videos make static images come alive.

Resource icons on each page help readers to further **explore key concepts**.

Published by AV2
350 5th Avenue, 59th Floor
New York, NY 10118
Website: www.av2books.com

Copyright ©2021 AV2

Library of Congress Control Number: 2019953672

ISBN 978-1-7911-1852-5 (hardcover)
ISBN 978-1-7911-1853-2 (softcover)
ISBN 978-1-7911-1854-9 (multi-user eBook)
ISBN 978-1-7911-1855-6 (single user eBook)

Printed in Guangzhou, China
1 2 3 4 5 6 7 8 9 0 24 23 22 21 20

032020
101319

Project Coordinator: Ryan Smith   Designer: Sushant Deshpande

Every reasonable effort has been made to trace ownership and to obtain permission to reprint copyright material. The publishers would be pleased to have any errors or omissions brought to their attention so that they may be corrected in subsequent printings.

AV2 acknowledges Getty Images, iStock, Shutterstock, and Alamy as its primary image suppliers for this title.

First published by North Star Editions in 2019.